THE TEA PARTY MANIFESTO

A Vision for an American Rebirth

BY JOSEPH FARAH

WND BOOKS

THE TEA PARTY MANIFESTO
A Vision for an American Rebirth
Published by WND Books, Inc.
Washington, D.C.

Written by Joseph Farah
Book designed by Mark Karis

WND Books are distributed to the trade by:
Midpoint Trade Books
27 West 20th Street, Suite 1102
New York, NY 10011

WND Books are available at special discounts for bulk
purchases. WND Books, Inc. also publishes books in electronic
formats. For more information call (541) 474-1776 or visit
www.wndbooks.com.

First Edition

ISBN 13 Digit: 978-1-935071-28-0
Library of Congress information available

Printed in the United States of America

10 9 8 7 6 5 4 3 2

TABLE OF CONTENTS

INTRODUCTION

THE TEA PARTY MOVEMENT is the most exciting, dynamic, powerful grassroots political movement of my lifetime.

It's a movement that arose spontaneously in the nick of time to save America from what seemed like a fatal drift off course from self-government and liberty.

But questions are arising about what is at the heart and soul of this movement.

For what exactly does the tea party movement stand?

It's a question you will see debated in the media and even among tea party activists themselves.

Since this movement arose quickly and spontaneously, without well-known and easily identifiable leaders, and without a founding document, it's not an easy question to answer.

Yet it is a question that must be answered if this movement is to grow, prosper, and be a continuing influence on the country in years to come — as I sincerely hope it will be.

After five years of running the most

successful, independent Internet news agency, WorldNetDaily — devoted to traditional American-style watchdog journalism, specializing in exposing fraud, waste, abuse, and corruption in government and powerful institutions — I found myself faced with a recurring question from visitors to the site:

"Thank you for exposing the *problems* we face as a nation, day after day, week after week. But how do we extricate ourselves as a people from the growing threat of government power grabs? What's the *solution?*"

The more I heard it, the more I began to take this frequent challenge seriously. It was difficult enough to investigate and expose the problems facing the nation in a daily news format. It was clear any effort to provide solutions to the pressing problems of the day would require a different venue, a different format.

So I began working on a book that could provide a coherent vision for individual action — one that would help answer those frequent questions from visitors to WND.

Taking America Back: A Radical Plan to Revive Freedom, Morality and Justice was first published in 2003, followed by a paperback edition. While the book's initial public reception wasn't spectacular, it became much more popular after the election of Barack Obama and the rise of the tea party movement that began in 2008.

When I was asked to be a keynote speaker, along with Sarah Palin, at the first national

Tea Party Convention in Nashville in 2010, the coordinator of the event, Judson Phillips, introduced me by saying, "He was a tea partier before there was a tea party movement."

Those words still make me smile today.

I do like to think my call for a popular uprising in America to hold government and other powerful institutions accountable to the rule of law and the will of the people helped in some way to trigger this movement, though I know that connection is tenuous at best.

I do believe, however, I can claim with some degree of accuracy to have predicted the rise of this movement.

In 2008, in my book *None of the Above: Why 2008 Is the Year to Cast the Ultimate Protest Vote*, I explained why neither of the two major-party candidates deserved to be president. I offered up two scenarios:

• The election of John McCain would mean the Democratic Congress would get most of what it wanted during his four-year term due to McCain's history of conciliation with the other party. As a result, the economy would continue to sputter out of control. But the Democratic Congress would not get the blame in 2010 and 2012. McCain would. There would be no popular uprising. Americans would be rightfully confused about who to blame. Democrats would likely gain more seats in Congress in 2010, and Barack Obama would likely win the presidency in 2012.

• The election of Barack Obama would mean Democrats would be in complete control of the White House and Congress. They would push through their radical agenda, which would cause a historic popular backlash.

Democrats would pay the price in the midterm election and, again, in 2012. But even more important than the political revolution would be the renewed engagement by citizenry — a development that could have the long-term impact of taking America back.

What I recognized was that McCain would not have set America on a right course. He supported the bailouts during the presidential race. He might have supported smaller bailouts in 2009, had he been elected. But he would most definitely not have provided principled opposition to the fundamental takeovers of the free-enterprise system.

The economy would still be in trouble — and guess who would be getting all the blame?

That's right. It would be the Republican president and Republicans in general. Although there would be bipartisan support for expansive and unconstitutional growth of the federal government, citizens would not be rising up attempting to reclaim their country through thousands of tea parties and other demonstrations. And there would be few viable alternatives for voters in the midterm congressional elections.

As the economy continued to stagger through 2012, McCain would be demonized for all the problems our country experienced in his four-year term, and Barack Obama would be getting ready for his first four years in office with a Congress stacked with even more Democrats and with even less opposition.

The only real difference would be that we delayed even greater pain for the country.

I believed, and still believe, America has a chance to wake up from its political sleepwalk. We needed to be jolted awake by experiencing the consequences of these horrendous policies, and Republicans had to be forced to rediscover their roots in and commitment to limited government.

For many Americans suffering right now through Obamanomics, it's probably still hard to imagine that John McCain would have offered, through his brand of bipartisan compromise, nothing but a scapegoat for Democrats to blame for their own policies — a scapegoat they will not have in 2010 and 2012.

On the other hand, people are waking up

all over this country — in just the first eighteen months of the Obama administration. They're seeing that socialism doesn't work. They're already marching in the streets by the millions. Ordinary, hard-working Americans who have never carried a protest sign in their lives are mobilized for action. America may never be the same.

Some thought I was crazy for saying that Obama could actually be a blessing in disguise for the future of our republic.

I recognized there would likely be more short-term pain under Obama. But I also predicted it would result in long-term gain.

The tea party movement arose from the disaster of 2008 to give us hope for a better future.

This book is about the promise of that movement.

It is about how tea party activists can best frame their arguments for widespread acceptance and long-lasting results. But, even more important, it is an effort toward defining a simple, coherent, articulate, visionary mission statement of broad appeal to Americans who are no longer content with the idea of leaving governance to politicians in Washington and state capitals.

CHAPTER 1: WHO WE ARE

I BELIEVE WITH ALL MY HEART that those in the trenches of the tea party movement have a well-grounded, fundamental understanding of the problems facing America:

  · That elected officials and bureaucrats in Washington are far exceeding the strict constitutional limits on their authority;

· That our major cultural institutions, which represent unelected, unaccountable, elite power centers — the major media, the entertainment industry, the major foundations, academia, the government education establishment, among others — are promoting bigger government and less freedom.

The tea party movement is *not*, as is often portrayed, a movement concerned only with materialistic economic issues — even if those issues were the straw that broke the camel's back and got so many individual activists into the streets.

In other words, it's not just about a collection of *issues* being debated in Washington — matters like health care, stimulus bills, corporate bailouts, and cap-and-trade legislation. Those are all critically important issues, but they hardly represent the totality of the tea party movement's grievances. In fact, those issues are more a symptom of the fundamental crises threatening America's very existence as a sovereign, free, vibrant, cohesive, self-governing nation-state.

Yet, I sense from some leaders of the tea party movement a reticence to venture outside that narrow focus — a focus that, quite honestly, obscures the forest for the trees.

It would be like trying to explain the dreams and aspirations of America's founders by confining them to material concerns like taxes. Anyone laboring under the delusion that the colonists' primary grievance was economic should immediately review the Declaration of Independence.

Their concerns were broadly set forth as "life, liberty and the pursuit of happiness." Their grievances were also individually itemized and few of them were economic. After all, the colonists, as I point out in *Taking America Back*, were doing quite well economically — probably better than the average Englishman.

But just as the founders had more in mind than economic prosperity, so should we, and so should the tea party movement.

The founders had a vision of an independent, self-governing, free nation that would safeguard inalienable individual rights under God. It was an unprecedented breakthrough for mankind. That vision represented a historic transformation. Because of the way that vision manifested itself into an independent nation, George Washington, whom Americans know as "the father of our nation," was known in the Europe of his time as "the father of freedom."

And this is the vision today's tea party movement needs to recreate if it is to take America back from the precipice — to revive liberty, restore social justice, and jump-start a moral renewal.

The founders were not afraid to talk in transcendent terms. They understood the risk in *not* doing so — in appealing only to people's narrow self-interest.

They understood that without feeling

accountable to God, men are incapable of governing themselves — which is, the founders taught us, the essence of liberty.

Today, some Americans are afraid of talking in spiritual terms. But the American Dream is under spiritual attack. So this is not a battle that can be won without acknowledging the rules of engagement. This is a spiritual battle — and if it is not fought in the spiritual realm, with prayer and obedience to God, then it will not be successful.

The heart and soul of the tea party movement is already there. The leaders of the tea party movement simply need to recognize it and encourage it.

Look at the signs at the massive, historic 9/12 rally in Washington:

"Resistance to tyrants is obedience to God."

"It's not about health care, it's about control!"

"Bring back the Constitution."

"One Nation Under God."

"Wake up America! Study the Constitution. It's the only thing between you and the tyranny of politicians."

"Wake up America – II Chronicles 7:14"

"Give me liberty or give me death!"

Yes, this is a broad coalition, but one whose concerns are not merely economic and material. Yes, this is a *radical* movement whose concerns transcend the economic and material. Yes, this is a reawakening of the American spirit that made this country good, great, and unique in history.

We sell it short by constraining it and defining it in almost purely economic and material terms.

There seems to be a fair amount of confusion over what the tea party movement is really all about.

I can tell you it is not about materialism. It is not simply about economics. And it is a mistake to assume it can be explained by polls on the most important "issues" from menus devised by tea party leaders.

There are groups and individuals who would like to constrict the tea party movement to fiscal issues.

That would be a huge mistake.

It's not just about government spending,

even though it was government spending that precipitated the unprecedented, spontaneous, grassroots uprising.

More precisely, it's about the law of the land and the will of the people.

It's about a nation whose government has lost its moorings.

It's about self-government.

And, fundamentally, it is about the Constitution and the Declaration of Independence.

Both tea party fans and detractors alike do a disservice to the movement, and underestimate it, by trying to suggest it's about this issue or that issue. Issues are fleeting. They change from day to day, week to week, month to month, and year to year. If this is going to be a movement that lasts, that transcends, that makes a far-reaching impact, it needs to get beyond the momentary and search deeply for meaning.

Here's how I define the tea party manifesto:

- Like America's forefathers, we believe we are accountable to a sovereign God who grants us unalienable rights to life, liberty, and the pursuit of happiness.

- Like America's forefathers, we believe the Constitution strictly limits the power of the federal government and uniquely recognizes and protects those unalienable individual rights.

That simple.

And, from my experience, it represents the

core values and beliefs of the overwhelming number of tea party participants and activists.

Are there atheists among the tea party crowd?

I'm sure there are. There were undoubtedly some atheists among America's founders. Nevertheless, they signed on to documents based on these two principles because they understood it represented perhaps the only true roadmap to liberty.

Did they also itemize their grievances with the Crown?

Sure they did.

But they didn't allow those individual grievances to divide them or to obscure their goal of self-government.

Neither must we.

Ultimately, as a people, we're either going to be accountable to God or we're going to be accountable to government.

As Bob Dylan said, "You gotta serve somebody."

If we are not accountable to God, we are incapable of self-government. The founders knew that. They were right. It's a biblical principle. It has been demonstrated a thousand times throughout history.

This is a time for first principles.

It's not just about health care or stimulus bills or bailouts or cap-and-trade or redistribution of wealth.

It's about life, liberty, and the pursuit of happiness.

If we want to redirect the country, we will

need to think beyond the immediate.

If you want a vision of what has motivated and energized millions of Americans to get off their rear ends and into the streets, you need to consider the vision our founders gave us in establishing this unique experiment in liberty.

That's a vision that can be and is being accepted by 99.9 percent of the tea party movement.

It's a beautiful vision. It's a unifying vision. It's a winning vision.

CHAPTER 2: DEFINING THE TERMS OF THE DEBATE

WHO IS THE TEA PARTY?

For what does it stand?

The conventional media stereotype is that the tea party movement is a right-wing phenomenon.

It is not.

There's much confusion about the meaning of left and right in America today.

The confusion is, ironically, on both the left and the right — and even in the middle.

Here's a simple way to think about the political spectrum that defies convention. But it just happens to be acutely accurate and commonsensical.

Let's start at the two extremes of the 180-degree political spectrum and work our way to the center.

On the left side is communism, which places all power in the hands of government. I think everyone can agree that communism is a left-wing philosophy.

What would be on the opposite end of a political spectrum from total government control? Obvious: No government. We have a word for proponents of no government. They are called anarchists. Thus, anarchists would be on the extreme right side of the political spectrum.

A true anarchist would be as far to the right as you can get on the political spectrum. To the left of anarchists would be libertarians, who acknowledge there is a role for government but want it strictly limited — often including no borders, no immigration laws, no laws prohibiting dangerous drugs, no laws preserving marriage between one man and one woman as the cornerstone of civilization, no laws restricting abortion.

Moving toward the center would be the philosophy that guided the founding of this country. It should also be the philosophy of the tea party movement. It's actually a centrist position on the political spectrum — not a right-wing position.

And who is over just to the left of us?

The people leading America on an inevitable march toward socialism — you might call them "soft socialists." They like to talk about a "mixed economy" in line with the European model.

The philosophy to the left of the "soft socialists" might surprise you if you've been indoctrinated into the conventional political spectrum model. It's called fascism, another brand of socialism.

Fascists don't insist that government own all the means of production. Fascists are content to control the means of production, not necessarily own it.

Right next to fascism on the extreme left side of the political spectrum is communism. It surprises many people to discover "fascists" are not right wing. But they are clearly not. In fact, it is a far left ideology. Fascism and communism are ideological kissing cousins. That's how close they are on the political spectrum and in their way of governance.

In fact, I would say that fascists are often mistakenly called communists. Take a look at China today and it is not by any stretch of the imagination communist. It is fascist. Even though most people who think of themselves as "left" would tell you they detest fascism, in practice they often do not.

Mussolini was beloved by the left and practically defined fascism. Hitler was embraced by the Communist Soviet Union, until he betrayed Stalin's non-aggression pact. Hollywood Communists led the "peace movement" in the United States and fought involvement in the European war *until* Hitler betrayed Stalin. Then, overnight, they became war mongers.

Anarchists are often described as left-wingers, when in fact they are on the extreme right of the political spectrum. Nazis and fascists are often labeled right-wingers, when in fact they are of the left. Again, the political spectrum, if it is to make any sense at all, should be based on attitude toward government.

Because of these misconceptions, many

Americans are missing the real political threat facing our country. It's not from communism, but it is from another form of socialism — fascism.

Whenever you hear about "public-private partnerships," you're hearing about a fascist concept.

Whenever you hear about emergency government plans to confiscate property, block transportation, and seize control of communications, it's a form of national socialism that is knocking on the door.

Look at the way we have abdicated our individual liberties in favor of "group rights." That's a fascist concept. Look at the way we demonize certain groups (whether you're talking about smokers or Bible-believing

Christians) and elevate others (Native Americans and homosexuals come to mind as the new noblemen or chosen people) in our society. That, too, is a fascist concept.

One of the reasons America is moving toward fascism today is because it has lost its moral bearings and its constitutional moorings. We're supposed to believe in limited government in the United States. The federal powers are enumerated in the Constitution. But, in recent years, Washington has far exceeded its authority. And very few politicians — Democrats or Republicans — seem to give a darn.

Just as many Americans don't understand the left-right political spectrum extends from totalitarian government control on the left to anarchy on the right, there's much confusion over the phony divide between "economic issues" and "social issues."

There are those who would like to stir up differences between evangelicals and the tea party movement — even while polls show evangelicals represent a large majority of tea party members.

There is pressure on the tea party movement to eschew "social issues." We have become conditioned to hearing that "social issues" are abortion and the gender-bending agenda. However, I would like to make the case that *all* political issues are, in fact, "social issues." And just as those entering the political fray as tea partiers should recognize this, so must the traditional "conservatives" who have focused their attention on abortion and gender-bending.

I have some familiarity with both camps.

The problem both have is not always seeing the forest for the trees.

America is not in trouble just because government no longer respects the sanctity of life and the sanctity of marriage. America is not in trouble just because government is spending more money than it has and because it is redistributing wealth. America is in trouble because government is doing all of these things and more to far exceed the strict limits of its constitutional authority.

And, just as importantly, America is in trouble because government has, to quote Aleksandr Solzhenitsyn, "forgotten God."

These are the two principles that *unite* the vast majority of the tea party movement with the more traditional "conservative" movement and especially those who are devoted to the sanctity of life and family.

There's no divide here.

There's only a divide if we create one — or if we fail to recognize the real divide.

And if we create one — or allow our enemies to create one — then America will return to business as usual, and the great awakening we have seen since 2008 will have been just a momentary blip on history's radar screen.

This is a time for unity among pro-life activists, pro-family activists, "conservative" activists, and libertarians. There are two

principles that unite most of these people —
whether they know it or not:

  • Overwhelmingly they believe we are accountable
  to a sovereign God who grants us unalienable
  rights to life, liberty, and the pursuit of happiness.

  • Overwhelmingly they believe the Constitution
  strictly limits the power of the federal
  government and uniquely recognizes and
  protects those unalienable rights.

Remember them. Commit them to
memory. Jot them down. Underline them.
These are the principles upon which this
movement is truly founded.

This is where the focus needs to be with
all of the freedom-oriented groups now
battling to take America back from those

who make it more like all the other nations of the world — those that long ago turned from God and those that don't have a 224-year-old Constitution that removed shackles from the people and placed them on the government.

I know the heart and soul of the tea party movement. It is populated by people who think just like I do about these big issues. It is a movement of prayerful people, people who love God, people who go to church and synagogue. And it is a movement of people who revere the Constitution. It is not just a movement founded upon issues of materialism and economics.

Remember, "all issues are social issues." The great economic plundering taking place by a rapacious government and the elite it serves is a "social issue." The victims are people. Private property rights constitute a "social issue." Equal protection under the law is a "social issue." The rule of law is a "social issue."

And, most of all, the will of the people is a "social issue."

Don't let your enemies dictate the terms of debate nor the rules of engagement.

If you care about life, liberty, and the pursuit of happiness, you care about "social issues."

Chapter 3: Not seeing the forest for the trees

AS I HAVE SAID, I *love* the tea party movement, and I think it is the greatest grassroots political uprising in America in my lifetime — not just in size, but in spirit.

But I have a warning for the rank-and-file activists, as well as the leaders.

It could easily go astray — even with all the best of motivations and intentions.

Let me give you an example.

Some of the tea party groups have been rallying behind an effort known as "The Contract *from* America."

The Contract *from* America, although undoubtedly well-intentioned, inadvertently does the movement a grave disservice — constraining it to concerns about relatively narrow issues, most of which are *materialistic*, rather than broad-stroke themes reminiscent of what America's first tea partiers, the founding fathers, drafted in 1776.

But you decide.

In 1776, the founders wrote the boldest vision for a future of independence, liberty, and self-government the world had ever seen — and none have rivaled its passion, its eloquence, or its primacy since:

"We hold these truths to be self-evident, that all men are created equal, that they are endowed by their Creator with certain unalienable Rights, that among these are Life, Liberty and the pursuit of Happiness. — That to secure these rights, Governments are instituted among Men, deriving their just powers from the consent of the governed, — That whenever any Form of Government becomes destructive of these ends, it is the Right of the People to alter or to abolish it, and to institute new Government, laying its foundation on such principles and organizing its powers in such form, as to them shall seem most likely to effect their Safety and Happiness," it said in part.

Yes, it's true the founders had some specific grievances that were stated plainly. But more importantly, the Declaration of Independence was a statement not so much about what the founders were *against* as what they were for — stated plainly, "life, liberty and pursuit of happiness."

They didn't limit their concerns to those that were economic. In fact, the colonists had it pretty good economically. True, they didn't appreciate taxation without representation, but they didn't say, "Look, it's the economy, stupid."

They made it clear that what they wanted was the freedom to govern themselves under God's authority. They didn't look for government to grant them favors. They spoke of being "endowed by their Creator with certain unalienable rights." Government was supposed to be in the business merely of *protecting* those rights, not granting them.

Look at the specific grievances. Few were economic in origin:

- Government was failing to do its job

- Government was exceeding its authority

- Government was violating individual rights

- Government was obstructing immigration laws

- Government was obstructing justice

- Government was turning the land into a police state

- Government was superseding the established laws of the land

Sound familiar?

That's exactly what Americans are enduring today at the hands of a government in Washington, not London.

Now let's compare those concerns with those of the proposed Contract *from* America:

- Demand a balanced budget

- Stop the tax hikes

- Pass market-based health care and health insurance reform

- Enact fundamental tax reform

- End runaway government spending

- Let us save

- Pass an "all-of-the-above" energy policy

- Restore fiscal responsibility and constitutionally limited government

- Protect private property rights

- Reject cap-and-trade

- Stop the pork

- Audit the Fed

- No more bailouts

- Stop career politicians and curb lobbyist power

- Sunset regulations and enact fundamental regulatory reform

That's not the complete list, but it represents most of the choices tea partiers are supposed to vote upon as the most important.

What do they have in common? They are all economic issues. They are all fundamentally "materialistic" concerns.

What's wrong with them? Nothing, as far

as they go. I'm all for them. Most of them are absolutely necessary if we are to become a prosperous country again. But is that all we want? Is that what the tea party movement is all about?

I don't think so.

The tea party movement shouldn't allow itself to be buried in a collection of individual, specific issues. That's not a broad vision of a future characterized by a return to self-government. This is simply *asking* an overreaching, out-of-control, and illegitimate central government to amend its economic priorities.

I have no doubts that the economic calamity this government wrought on the people ignited this movement spontaneously. However, we've got to think beyond materialism.

A movement like this needs a spiritual core.

And I believe it has one — it just simply is not reflected in this document.

When I attend tea party gatherings and rallies, I hear that spirit from the attendees. I see it in their signs. I feel it in their hearts and souls. But it's missing from this document.

This document limits the yearnings of what I see, hear, and feel.

I know where this comes from. It emanates from the desire to build a "big tent."

Does that sound familiar?

It does to me. It has repeatedly been the mistake of the Republican Party, which eschewed "social issues" in favor of economic issues and materialistic concerns.

That was a mistake then. And this is a mistake now.

In fact, the very idea of "social issues" was a fabrication from the start. As I said, all issues are "social issues." All issues are moral issues. Taxation, limited government, trade laws — all are moral issues.

Understand that I am not interested in *expanding* the list of issues. I am proposing narrowing it — just as the founders did.

We can all quibble about this issue or that issue. But we can all unite on two principles:

· That we have an established Constitution that governs our affairs as the basis for the rule of law in this country and it must be observed both in letter and in spirit;

• That we seek to live as a self-governing people with accountability to God, not government, and have the right today, as yesterday, to pursue "life, liberty and the pursuit of happiness."

That's it.

Why do we need to say more?

That's a broad banner. Those are proclamations that will lead to building the biggest tent ever. That's a statement of principle that will ensure this movement is blessed and long-lasting and effective.

Don't allow the tea party movement to be sold short.

Don't repeat the mistakes of the past.

Don't constrain the vision to materialistic ambitions.

As the founders understood and stated so eloquently, only a moral people with knowledge and reverence for God's role in our lives can ever be capable of self-government.

I still believe what the Bible says in 2 Chronicles 7:14: "If my people, which are called by my name, shall humble themselves, and pray, and seek my face, and turn from their wicked ways; then will I hear from heaven, and will forgive their sin, and will heal their land."

How about you?

I don't raise these points to engage in conflict with anyone from the tea party movement. I raise them to strengthen it, to embolden it, and to ensure that it is successful — for the long-term.

I raise them because the very future of our nation is at stake.

CHAPTER 4: THE MEANING OF INDEPENDENCE

WHAT'S GOING ON HERE?

• Dozens of governors, legislatures, and state attorneys general are suing the federal government to stop the enforcement of unconstitutional legislation like the so-called "health-care reform bill."

• More than a dozen state legislatures have, in one form or another, asserted their states' independence and sovereignty, making it clear they are not subservient to the whims of Washington.

• Several states have exempted themselves from federal firearms restrictions.

• The governor of Texas hinted at the possibility of seceding from the United States if the federal government insisted on meddling in its internal affairs.

Something is happening here in the United States — something unprecedented in the last 150 years.

And it's a good something.

States are telling the federal government to take a hike. They are reminding

Washington, the man with the gun, that they are sovereign states, not subjects of the central government. They are explaining to Uncle Sam that the Constitution strictly limits the powers of the federal government and reserves all non-enumerated authority to the states.

There's something happening here, indeed.

And it's not just a reaction to overreaching from the federal government. It's actually the solution to many of our political problems.

What Washington has been doing for the last 150 years, and particularly in the last fifty, is totally *unsustainable*.

Sustainability is a word "progressives" love. They use it mostly to talk about the environment. The irony is that nature takes care of itself. It's man's systems that are unsustainable — especially when they involve massive accumulations and centralizations of wealth, power, and debt. Those systems cannot be sustained.

Just as the tea party movement is a natural reaction to the abuses and illegality of a federal government exceeding its authority, so, too, is the state sovereignty movement.

This one is taking place largely below the radar screen of the national media and the awareness of the general population.

Every one of these actions is being taken with full awareness of the implications. States are embarking on these courses with the knowledge of what they are up against — legal challenges and, ultimately, superior force.

That two movements of this kind have materialized — one fighting for individual rights and self-government under the Constitution and the other for states' rights and state sovereignty under the Constitution — is not only historic, it's the roadmap to victory and liberty and possibly another 100 years of U.S. prosperity.

It's a rekindling of the spirit that birthed this country. It's a rebirth of the ideals that made it great. It's a revival of the energy that vigilantly sustained it.

The tea party movement needs to embrace what's happening in the states. It needs to engage in it, support it, stand with governors, legislatures, and other officials who stand up to Washington and stand for the Constitution.

There's power in the states. Unfortunately, until very recently, most state officials didn't realize it — or, perhaps, they knew it and chose to sell out in the face of Washington's bribes and coercion. The Constitution makes clear that the federal government has very little actual authority. Its powers are strictly limited. State power, however, is not so limited. The powers of the states are limited only by their own constitutions and by the will of their people.

If you want to bring Washington to accountability, you need to do it in two ways — by electing responsible members of Congress who will honor and adhere to the letter and spirit of the Constitution, and to keep the federal government in check through the power of the states.

Those courageous state officials standing up to Washington's excesses need the support of the people. Who better to give them that support than the tea party movement?

independence: freedom from control or influence of another or others

At this writing, it has been 234 years since the drafting and signing by America's founders of our national birth certificate, the Declaration of Independence.

That's why some of us — too few, really — call the holiday we commemorate every year on July 4 "Independence Day." That is, indeed, the actual name of the holiday.

It's not just the Fourth of July. It's not just the day we shoot off Chinese-made fireworks, barbecue burgers, and go to the beach. It's Independence Day — so named because on or about this date in 1776, a group of courageous men risked their lives, their fortunes, and their sacred honor for a dream of freedom and sweet autonomy from an imperial power.

We ought to mark this occasion with some real reflection — even some solemnity and sobriety.

Unfortunately, too few Americans today put much value in independence. Most no longer celebrate, cherish, or appreciate independence. Independence is not considered an ideal.

Our political and cultural elite don't want to see a nation full of independent-minded, self-governing citizens who will hold their leaders accountable to their will and the laws of the land. They would prefer sheep. So they have conspired to bring into America millions and millions more sheep — illegally.

You will hear the elite preach about the value of living in an "interdependent" world. Have you heard that? "Interdependence" — this is considered a good thing. Keep in mind every time you hear the word "interdependence" glorified and revered that interdependence is simply a synonym for "dependence."

It has nothing to do with "independence"

— that thing for which our founders risked and sacrificed everything.

The sad truth is the American dream of independence has been betrayed. Americans are worse off today, in terms of individual freedom, than they were before the War of Independence. In fact, take a look at the dictionary definition of "colony" and see if it doesn't apply to us today.

colony: 1) a group of people who settle in a distant land but remain under the political jurisdiction of their native land 2) a territory distant from the state having jurisdiction or control over it

Aren't Americans, in a sense, all colonists of the great imperial throne in the District of

Columbia? We all pay tribute to this faraway empire. We are, in reality, little more than serfs doing the bidding of those in the federal corridors of power in Washington. We're taxed without real representation. We're forced to support a growing standing army of federal police in our communities. And we face a growing threat of disarmament — one of the great fears of the colonists who touched off the American Revolution at Lexington and Concord.

What do you think?

Are we better off today than our forefathers were in 1776?

Are we living freer lives today than the founders were?

If George Washington and Thomas

Jefferson could return today to see America — the tax rates, the overreaching central government, the subservience of states to Washington, the non-limitations on the federal government — would they consider us free? Would they consider us independent?

Is American sovereignty and independence still worth a fight?

What are you willing to risk? What are you willing to sacrifice today in the name of freedom and independence?

America's War of Independence was a unique conflict in the history of the world. While there have been countless independence movements designed to throw off the shackles of foreign control, this one was also designed to throw off the shackles that all governments tend to place on the people, while deliberately placing shackles on the newly designed independent government.

That's what the U.S. Constitution represents — the first and only time in history when men threw off the chains of slavery and servitude and placed them on the government.

No longer would men be ruled by government. Instead there would be a government of the people, by the people, and for the people. Men would govern themselves under the rule of law.

It was a breakthrough vision, a *radical* vision. It was truly, from man's viewpoint, a *revolutionary* vision.

Where did our founders get the concept?

They got their inspiration from another radical document — the Bible.

Today, many pastors, church leaders, and theologians have a more timid view of biblical faith in the public square. Some even subscribe to the view that the Bible provides a blanket condemnation of resistance to tyranny.

The contention that believers should simply lay down and comply with even the most hideous requirements of government is an old argument. It was thoroughly debated by America's Christian founders when they took up arms to defend their Declaration of Independence in 1776 — and even before at Lexington and Concord when British troops tried to take away their arms.

Many of the founders were biblical scholars

— and well aware of Paul's warning in Romans
13:1-7, most often the text cited by the new
defenders of the "divine right of kings":

Let every soul be subject unto the higher
powers. For there is no power but of God: the
powers that be are ordained of God. Whosoever
therefore resisteth the power, resisteth the
ordinance of God: and they that resist shall
receive to themselves damnation. For rulers are
not a terror to good works, but to the evil. Wilt
thou then not be afraid of the power? do that
which is good, and thou shalt have praise of
the same: For he is the minister of God to thee
for good. But if thou do that which is evil, be
afraid; for he beareth not the sword in vain: for
he is the minister of God, a revenger to execute
wrath upon him that doeth evil. Wherefore ye
must needs be subject, not only for wrath, but
also for conscience sake. For for this cause pay
ye tribute also: for they are God's ministers,

attending continually upon this very thing. Render therefore to all their dues: tribute to whom tribute is due; custom to whom custom; fear to whom fear; honour to whom honour.

I believe we profoundly dishonor our heroic and inspired founders when we accuse them of disobeying Paul's admonition and an even more grave disservice to the Word of God when we read too much into seven verses in one book of the Bible to the exclusion of the complete context of its sixty-six books.

To me it is clear Paul was exhorting us not to overthrow government *as an institution*, because it was ordained by God. However, this passage in no way suggests that believers are simply to submit to unjust laws.

That the founders were not anarchists was

demonstrated by the speed with which they acted to form a new government in the very act of declaring their independence from a foreign power that had refused to negotiate further with them on their legitimate grievances. They recognized government was, in a fallen world, a necessary evil.

But the Bible is also teeming with acts of civil disobedience and deliverance from tyranny — so much so that they inspired not just the founders but men like Martin Luther King, Jr.

I think of Pharaoh's daughter and Moses' mother in Exodus 2.

I think of Meshach, Shadrach and Abednego in Daniel 3.

I think of Moses himself in Exodus 2

when he killed an Egyptian who was beating a Hebrew slave.

I think of Daniel praying in defiance of the king in Daniel 6.

How about Abraham, who mounted an army of several hundred men and took on four kings who had captured his nephew Lot? For laying waste to those kingdoms he was toasted by Melchizedek, king of Salem, in Genesis 14.

I could go on and on, but let me give you one striking example of the way the Bible actually celebrates heroes of the faith who take extraordinary, even violent actions to liberate themselves from ungodly rulers.

The Book of Judges recounts ancient Israel's frequent temptations to disobey

God and pay the consequences and then to cry for a deliverer — with their prayers heard.

Such was the case with Ehud, son of Gera, a left-handed Benjamite who actually assassinated Eglon, the ruler of the Israelites' conquerors, the Moabites, in a story told in Judges 3.

"And he said unto them, Follow after me: for the LORD hath delivered your enemies the Moabites into your hand. And they went down after him, and took the fords of Jordan toward Moab, and suffered not a man to pass over. And they slew of Moab at that time about ten thousand men, all lusty, and all men of valour; and there escaped not a man. So Moab was subdued that day under the hand of Israel. And the land had rest fourscore years."

In Romans 13, Paul was not suggesting that any earthly kings or rulers have absolute authority and God's blessing to torment their subjects, oppress God's people, break covenants, or, most importantly, ignore God's laws.

Our founders believed — and I think they were right — that when King George broke his own laws, he was acting without authority. The same principle applies today to our own leaders when they break trust with the Constitution and God's laws.

There's a warning for them in Psalm 149:5-9:

"Let the saints be joyful in glory: let them sing aloud upon their beds.

Let the high praises of God be in their mouth, and a two-edged sword in their hand;

To execute vengeance upon the heathen, and punishments upon the people;

To bind their kings with chains, and their nobles with fetters of iron;

To execute upon them the judgment written: this honour have all his saints. Praise ye the LORD."

Bind our kings with chains and their nobles with fetters of iron?

Could this be where our founders got the idea of removing the chains from the people and placing them on the government?

It could be.

George Washington and the other founders of this once-great country came up with something quite new in the history of the world — the idea of self-governance. They not only threw off the yoke of foreign domination, but they invented a political system that took the shackles off the people and placed them where they belong — on central government.

What they created was so powerful and awe-inspiring, we need look nowhere else for role models today. We don't need to create something new. We need only to find our way to rediscovering what we had, something that was perverted over time and today is under full-scale assault.

Today, counter-revolutionaries are running the show in America. They have subverted much of what the founders bestowed upon us. The counter-revolutionaries in Washington and elsewhere are the lawless ones. They are the ones who are perverting justice and morality and order.

If the founders' legacy is to have meaning in the future of America, we need to become resistance fighters. We need to become tea party patriots. We need to become the new Minutemen. We need to be willing to sacrifice our comfort — maybe even our lives, our fortunes, and our sacred honor.

The very will of the American people is under attack in a thousand ways. It's under attack through the popular culture with its desensitizing images and messages. It's under attack from the establishment press, whose members think they are so much wiser than the simple rubes who work hard, provide for their families, and serve their country faithfully and heroically in times of national emergency. It's under attack from high priests in black robes who issue decrees that make a disgrace of the concept of the rule of law and mock the will of the people. It's under attack from elitists who run major foundations. It's under attack from globalists who seek to destroy America's national sovereignty. And it's under attack from a central government that has broken the shackles deliberately placed on it just over 200 years ago by our Constitution.

The onslaught is coming fast and furious from these enemies of liberty.

They are attempting to overwhelm the will of the people and the rule of law by setting political and cultural brushfires from coast to coast. They believe they have an opportunity to reach their goals for conquest of the American spirit in the short term, and they don't want to miss this opportunity.

Many Americans are indeed dispirited as a result. They look around and they no longer recognize their country and what it is rapidly becoming.

But I remain hopeful that these dark forces have so blatantly overstepped their authority, acting precipitously and rashly, and overreached toward their insidious and evil goals.

What they have managed to do is

awaken a slumbering giant — Americans' determination to remain free.

I see it in the faces of the much-maligned tea party protesters and those waving the America flag. I see it in those millions of American families dropping out of the system and homeschooling their children, and in those buying guns and ammunition in record numbers. I see it in the million bloggers — the new pamphleteers — meticulously documenting the wave of crimes being perpetrated in boardrooms, courtrooms, legislative chambers, executive suites, newsrooms, and oval offices.

I see it in the faces of a new activism percolating up from the grass roots, and in the countless Americans determined to be more responsible as their so-called leaders demonstrate almost incomprehensible irresponsibility.

I see it in the state officials who are proclaiming the sovereign rights and powers specifically reserved for them in the Constitution.

It gives me hope. It gives me encouragement. It gives me the idea that the American Dream is not yet dead.

But it's not enough to stabilize the situation. We can't return to business as usual. The policies and drift of recent years need to reversed. We need to do a 180. We need to take back ground.

That's the challenge and opportunity the tea party movement has before it.

It's not enough to cut taxes, to slow the inevitable trend toward socialism, and to throw the current rascals out.

It's time to reclaim the promise our founders gave us uniquely in the Declaration of Independence and the Constitution. It's time for a complete renewal of liberty, justice, and morality.

It's time for a vision as bold as the one that launched this great country.

Chapter 5: Don't Wait for Political Messiahs

TO BE PERFECTLY HONEST, when I wrote my book *Taking America Back* in 2003, Republicans weren't really excited about it. After all, Republicans controlled the presidency and both houses of Congress.

They believed they had already taken

America back.

Only now are many of them awakening to the realization that freedom-loving, moral people actually lost ground during the years with Republicans in control of the legislative and executive branches of government.

I expected this. In fact, I wrote in *Taking America Back* that this would happen even if Republicans controlled every seat in the House of Representatives and Senate and the White House.

There are several reasons for this:

• Most Republicans do not necessarily honor, revere, and abide by the Constitution;

• Most Republicans are not committed to rolling back the advances of socialism and immorality that have overtaken the country over the last fifty years of American history;

• Even if most Republicans were committed to such a goal, the courts and America's key cultural institutions are actively pushing another agenda and slowly, inevitably changing the hearts and minds of the people to accept un-American values of collectivism and moral relativism.

Some have begun to say, "I'm not a Republican, I'm a *conservative*." Personally, I prefer one the founders used themselves — "patriot." I'm also very much at home in the tea party movement. So please feel free to call me a tea partier. I'm honored by that label.

But labels have limited value. One-word slogans do not move people. If they did, socialism would not be advancing because few Americans identify with it. If they did, immorality would not be advancing because few Americans identify with it.

What conservative activists need to understand — because they are good people who need to be involved in the constructive process of moving the country forward — is that politicians follow; they do not lead.

It's up to the conservative activists to reorient themselves, reinvent themselves in light of the political, social, and cultural realities of the twenty-first century. It's time for them to join the tea party movement — if they haven't already.

Ronald Reagan was a wonderful man. He's one of my heroes. He was a blessing to this country and the world because he momentarily slowed down the trend toward tyranny and immorality. We can learn much from him. But he's dead and gone. And there are no more Ronald Reagans on the horizon, as far as I can see.

Moreover, even if another Reagan did come along, we must recognize that there are no political messiahs who can revive freedom, morality, and justice in America. At best, they can only point the way.

Most of that work needs to be done outside the political arena — way outside. It needs to be done in our homes, in our neighborhoods, in our communities, in our churches and synagogues, in our cultural institutions.

It's great that we learned from Ronald Reagan and were inspired by him; now it's time to learn from our adversaries who are inexorably advancing their causes daily — in election years and non-election years.

How do they do it?

They've won the culture. That's the ultimate battleground. It's the Ho Chi Minh trail to political power.

Also, and even more importantly, we need to learn from our Founding Fathers who, along with building a new political institution, built great cultural institutions to support them — the free press, great colleges and universities, churches that took care of widows and orphans and helped the needy.

We need to look to their example. These men were risk-takers. They were willing to try something that had never been tried before in the history of mankind. They were truly revolutionaries — not in the subversive way we think of revolutionaries today, but in the best sense of the word, like the prophets of old who were willing to challenge the establishment even if it meant their deaths.

Those who understand the importance of these things need to discover more effective ways to reach others, to communicate with them, to persuade them about right and wrong and the ultimate issues of life.

Changing times call for changing strategies. And the election of 2008 has persuaded innumerable freedom-loving people that times have indeed changed. Business as usual will not be enough to preserve the last vestiges of liberty in

America. It will certainly not be enough to *expand* liberty, morality, and justice in America – and that should be our goal.

Conservatism is a purely defensive political movement for a more innocent time, a time when our most basic constitutionally protected liberties were not being stripped from us – a time when government was not greatly exceeding its authority at the expense of personal freedom, social justice, and the Judeo-Christian values necessary to self-governance.

The tea party movement must not fall victim to the same temptation to be exclusively "defensive" in nature. It especially needs to guard against the temptation to limit itself to economic and material concerns.

As an onslaught of legislation and government action continues — legislation and action designed to attack our national independence and sovereignty, redistribute wealth not only domestically but internationally, strangle dissent and freedom of speech, take away our right to bear arms and fundamentally pervert the Constitution through legislation, executive action and judicial activism, it's time for freedom-loving Americans to go on offense. It's time not for timidity and civility and traditional conservatism. It's time for a much more radical, bold, and courageous approach to taking America back.

This new movement has a successful precedent in American history. It was the radical, patriotic, revolutionary movement of our colonial fathers. It launched the greatest experiment in liberty the world has ever known.

That should be our model. Nothing else will do. Our founders set out to separate themselves from those who oppressed them, from those who denied them their God-given human rights, from those who broke the law. They did this against all odds. They did this without concern about the popularity of their movement, only its rightness. And, with God's help, they succeeded, providing inspiration for people around the world for the last two centuries.

It's time to declare your independence.

The time for mere debate is over. The

facts are clear. We have no one else to blame for our troubles if we refuse to take responsibility for our own lives and show our neighbors there is a better way — through self-governance and personal responsibility.

I don't suggest it will be easy. It wasn't easy for our founders. They risked everything. It's time for contemporary freedom lovers and freedom fighters to do the same.

One more thing: Don't sit around waiting for a leader to emerge to start the movement and to give you marching orders. *YOU* are the leader. *YOU* are in charge of your family. *YOU* need to practice self-government if you want to see self-government spread. *YOU* are the leader you have been waiting for.

Make change happen in your life, in

your family, in your community and that movement will spread like wildfire across this country.

It's already happening. The tea party movement is proof.

CHAPTER 6: THE OPPOSITE OF CONSTITUTION IS PROSTITUTION

ACCORDING TO HIS dwindling number of supporters, Barack Obama is a constitutional legal scholar.

He taught constitutional law at the University of Chicago Law School for ten years. He often references this credential in touting his own knowledge and understanding of the Constitution.

But what does he really know about the U.S. Constitution?

How does he actually view it?

Does he see the Constitution as the framers did, binding the authority of the federal government?

Or does he take the view prevalent in most U.S. universities and law schools today that the Constitution is a "living, breathing document" that adapts to changing times, conditions, and mores?

You don't need to be a "scholar" to understand the Constitution. It was written to be easily understood by ordinary people —

ranchers and farmers and men who worked with their hands in the eighteenth century. In addition to leaving us with the final document, the framers left us with hundreds of pages of writings about the debates they had with each other over the drafting and ratification process.

There can be little mistake about what they meant, what they had in mind, what they were thinking and why, if you take the time to read the Constitution and those papers.

The legal debate today is over whether we should follow the letter and spirit of the Constitution, or whether it is merely a symbolic guidepost whose meaning can be changed by the clever arguments of attorneys and judges.

Is it really necessary for us to take seriously the restrictions the Constitution places on the powers of the federal government?

To that all-important question, I'm afraid the unequivocal answer from Barack Obama is a resounding "no."

Let me quote his own words, from pages 92-93 of *The Audacity of Hope*:

"What the framework of our Constitution can do is organize the way by which we argue about our future. All of its elaborate machinery — its separation of powers and checks and balances and federalist principles and Bill of Rights — are designed to force us into a conversation, a 'deliberative democracy' in which all citizens are required to engage in a process of testing their ideas against an external reality, persuading others of their point of view, and building shifting alliances of consent. Because power in our government is so diffuse, the process of making law in America compels us to entertain the possibility that we are not always right and to sometimes change our minds; it challenges us to examine our motives and our interests constantly, and suggests that both our individual and collective judgments are at once legitimate and highly fallible."

What does that mean?

Not much, I'm afraid.

Considering the man taught constitutional law at a major university, the lack of clarity and precision in this written statement is astounding and somewhat alarming.

There's not much substance here, at all. It's not much more than gibberish. But let me attempt to decipher it.

The long and short of it, as far as I can tell, is this: "The Constitution is not the binding law of the land. Instead, it is a framework for stimulating debate — a guidepost for testing our ideas."

In other words, Barack Obama reads the Constitution like he reads the Bible. Both, he believes, contain some good ideas. But no one should take either too literally.

Obama talked about the kind of judges he would appoint — especially to the U.S. Supreme Court. We all understand, or should, the job of a judge is to interpret the law, not make it. The role of the judge is to apply the law without fear or favor. The judge is not supposed to bend and twist the law to shape an agenda.

Yet, consider what Obama is looking for in his judicial appointments: "We need somebody who's got the heart, the empathy, to recognize what it's like to be a young teenage mom. The empathy to understand what it's like to be poor, or African-American, or gay, or disabled, or old. And that's the criteria by which I'm going to be selecting my judges."

Those are nice sentiments, indeed — but altogether rather narrow, don't you think?

For instance, I'd also like to see judges appointed who have empathy for people who work hard, keep their families together, obey the law, and contribute to their communities. I don't see many federal judges or members of Congress who have much of an appreciation for people like that and the sacrifice and commitment it requires.

More to the point, Barack Obama is speaking here in code. He is telling his constituency that he is going to appoint judges who will continue to transform the Constitution from the document designed to shackle the government to one that frees Washington to do whatever it wants, whenever it wants.

In other words, he intends to unshackle the government from constitutional restraints. Of course, when you unshackle government power from constitutional restraints, those shackles, as the framers understood, tend to wind up restraining liberty.

CHAPTER 7: SHOULD THE TEA PARTY BE A POLITICAL PARTY?

SOMETIMES THOSE OF US who have been around awhile take too much for granted.

I tend to assume, for instance, that most Americans understand socialism is an evil, immoral system of economics and government.

But with all the miseducation taking place in our schools and universities, it's worth getting back to basics.

What's wrong with socialism?

What's wrong with the government running things, ruling people, calling the shots, solving the problems, grabbing power it is forbidden from grabbing?

- Do you believe in private property?

- How would you feel if someone took yours?

- Where has socialism ever succeeded?

- What does the government do well?

- What does the Bible have to say about economics?

- What did America's founders have to say about economics?

- Is socialism constitutional?

I find the answers to these questions are often enough to persuade well-meaning, moral people that socialism is a disaster.

Most people believe in private property — especially their own.

Most people don't like having their things stolen. In fact, it's government's job to protect you from theft, not to be the thief.

Most people will be unable to point to a single successful socialist experiment — unless they choose some relatively new Western nation with a "mixed economy." Those include Canada, formerly Great Britain, France, and other European countries. You could even include the United States in this category. It's important to recognize that mere survival as a nation over a period of time does not make for a successful experiment. Socialism, for instance, aims to eliminate or reduce poverty. In none of these nations has poverty been eliminated or reduced as a result of socialist experiments.

Most people recognize that government is an inherently inefficient beast. What they might not recognize is that it also poses the greatest threat to freedom. The more power it has, the less freedom individual citizens have. Government is a necessary evil — something that should be tolerated as a limited nuisance, not counted on for your basic needs.

Most people don't realize the Bible countenances private property. It holds it up as honorable — as long as it does not become a diversion from God, as long as it does not become man's god.

Most people apparently forget what our founders had to say about property. They forget that our Constitution expressly limits the power of the federal government. You could say constitutionally limited government is the opposite of socialism.

That's how Obama got elected. Because words alone are often not enough to persuade anyone against mankind's innate desire to collectivize and rebel against God's order.

It often takes strong medicine to cure people of their infectious flirtation with socialism. In America, I believe that medicine, believe it or not, is named Barack Obama.

Think about it.

Who birthed this movement?

Barack Obama did — just as I predicted his election would back in 2008.

It's a reaction to Obama's efforts to remake the United States of America in his own image — socialist, utopian, globalist, secular, humanist.

The broad rejection of Obama's policies, and those of Nancy Pelosi and Harry Reid, is the essence of what the tea party movement is all about.

But there's more to it than defensiveness and rejection. At its core, the tea party is a recommitment by tens of millions of Americans to the Constitution of the United States, the Declaration of Independence, and the vision of the founders.

While elements of the conservative movement have emphasized the Constitution, the rule of law, and the will of the people, conservatives have traditionally lacked the fiery commitment to that document that I see among tea partiers.

And this is another reason why the tea party movement has so much more potential for growth and sustainability than does the more conservative movement.

The basis of the tea party movement is outraged that Washington, including both Democrat and Republican politicians, has allowed the Constitution to be shredded. It has seldom been invoked to limit the authority and reach of Washington into the lives of American citizens and the fifty states.

When all is said and done, the tea party is about the Constitution. It's about the rule of law, not the rule of men. It's about the will of the people, not the will of the Washington elite.

It's not about this issue or that issue. It's not about a grab bag of grievances. It's about the Constitution.

In a short time, this movement has far outgrown the modern conservative movement in its fifty-year history. And it has done so for two reasons: Barack Obama, and the simplicity of the tea party movement's agenda — reaffirmation of the rule of law and the will of the people.

The tea party movement has already eclipsed the conservative movement in size and strength. It has energized millions of Americans who have never before been engaged in politics.

So where does it go from here?

First some words of caution from an admiring observer:

• Don't look to veteran politicians for expertise. Often, but not always, they have as part of their agenda personal self-empowerment rather than setting our country on the right course.

• Don't look to politicians as your saviors. This is a nation founded on the principle of "self-government," meaning we govern ourselves, not rule by elites in state capitals or in Washington.

• Get involved personally, not just in conferences and rallies and marches, but in the political process at the grassroots level — precinct organizing, local party politics, city and county elections. This is the fertile ground upon which the future harvest of citizen-leaders emerges.

• Always remember what you believe — that the Constitution and the Declaration of Independence represent the entire framework of American government. Don't add to it. Don't subtract from it.

How do we take America back? Do we work within the Republican Party or the conservative movement? Or do we form a new political party — the Tea Party?

This may sound crazy, but I think both of those ideas are thinking too small.

Yes, working within the Republican Party in 2010 represents the quickest way to make an immediate impact on Washington's efforts to steal away our liberties. It is probably the best vehicle for continued redirection in 2012. But what's wrong with having *both* major political parties committed to the Constitution? Shouldn't any viable political party in America be sworn to upholding the spirit and letter of the Constitution?

Unlike the conservative movement, the tea party movement has a chance to accomplish that goal. And it ought to embrace as a goal the deliberate takeover of *both* parties by the midterm elections of 2014.

I know that's a super-ambitious goal. But all it takes is the manpower and determination the tea party movement has already demonstrated.

Can you imagine how beautiful America would be if *both* political parties were actually committed to preserving constitutionally limited government?

The conservative movement could never have achieved that objective.

But the tea party movement can.

Both major parties are there for the taking. They are controlled by a limited number of activists. This uprising that has occurred in the last year should be a signal to us all that we don't have to be satisfied with having one of the two American political parties committed to preserving America. We can and should have them both.

Wouldn't it be nice if the two major political parties in America fought over minor issues rather than fundamental structural issues? Wouldn't it be nice if both parties were committed to observing the Constitution? And if both actually wrangled over how to empower individuals and states rather than promoting bigger and more intrusive central government?

You bet it would.

And only when we have them both will we be able to ensure there's no going back to unconstitutional government in America.

We've experienced it and we don't like it.

Who would have imagined Obama would be responsible for undoing all for which he stood?

Our education has come. It came from the inevitably failed policies of Obama and his party. It has been a painful awakening.

That's what's wrong with socialism.

People have to see it for themselves.

They have to experience the misery and the control.

They have to see it with their own eyes.

And we are seeing it now.

Maybe someday we can find it in our hearts to thank Obama for this awakening. But not now. Now is the time for reclaiming our country.

Now is the time for getting America back on track.

Now is the time to summon enough courage and desire to fight to regain what we have lost.

CHAPTER 8: SO WHAT DO WE DO?

Whenever the founders faced a tough decision or a seemingly insurmountable challenge, history shows what they did.

Whether it was George Washington freezing with his colonial army at Valley Forge or disagreements arising at the constitutional convention, America's founders petitioned the Almighty for divine providence.

No matter what we call ourselves today — tea party activists, conservatives, freedom fighters, or patriotic Americans — we need to do the same thing.

We cannot divorce ourselves from the transcendent. Our best ideas for freedom will be like filthy rags before the God of the universe if we don't commit ourselves and our works to Him.

That's my very best advice to anyone who wants to take America back.

We don't just need to take back America's economic system. We don't just need to take back America's prosperity. We don't just need to take back America's laws. We don't just need to take back America's political system. We need to take back America's soul — and we need to do it in a way that will please God.

I understand that not everyone believes in God.

I understand that some people are offended by invocations of God.

I understand that some people would prefer to avoid divisions that can arise because of God.

Nevertheless, if we want to succeed, we need to be blessed by God.

George Washington knew it. Benjamin Franklin knew it. Thomas Jefferson knew it. John Adams knew it. James Madison knew it.

If they needed His help, so do we.

Just as Gideon learned, I'd rather have a smaller army with God on my side than the largest army in the world devoid of God.

People need something to believe in that is greater than themselves and their wallets. Nothing great was ever accomplished in world history by men motivated by materialism and economics alone.

An economics-only agenda won't build the bigger tent that some envision by avoiding controversial moral issues. The tea party movement needs to embrace a clear, simple, and profound message — and there is none better than the rallying cry of our founders: "Life, liberty and the pursuit of happiness."

More specifically, here is the two-point mission statement I would put forward for the tea party movement:

> • That we have an established Constitution that governs our affairs as the basis for the rule of law in this country and it must be observed both in letter and in spirit;

> • That we seek to live as a self-governing people with accountability to God, not government, and have the right today, as yesterday, to pursue "life, liberty and the pursuit of happiness."

Simple.

It worked before. It will work again.

Why reinvent the wheel?

Why turn our beliefs into a popularity contest on the issues of the day?

Our political adversaries have made clear they have no room for God in their plans.

They have made government their god. That's one of the principal dividing points between us. We need to say it — and mean it.

If we're afraid to say it and don't mean it, this movement will not be blessed.

"Government is not the solution to our problem," Ronald Reagan told us. "Government *is* the problem."

He was right. But it's not the only problem.

It's not just the government that has been stolen from the people. Today, the family, the very building block of Western civilization, is under siege. Can we afford to ignore that fact? We do so at our own peril.

The best thing we can do to protect and defend the family is to do everything possible to strengthen our own. That means loving one another. But it also means training up our children in the ways of the Lord. It does not mean turning them over to the state for indoctrination.

Can any of us truly be free if life itself is not defended in our society? I don't see how. Yet today life at both ends of the spectrum — young and old, healthy and infirm — is under attack. Is prosperity a higher calling for us than the defense of life? Can any of us truly be free if the innocent are condemned to death?

We have much work to do in taking back America's political institutions. But we must never overlook the power of America's *cultural* institutions in shaping opinion —

the free press, institutions of learning, foundations, churches, the entertainment media. Political power, if reclaimed, will fall right back into the hands of the enemy if we are not successful in supporting the few non-statist, God-fearing, pro-American alternatives and founding new ones.

The enemy controls the culture. We must take it back.

It may seem like a mission impossible. It may seem like the odds are against us. It may seem like there is too much to do.

But we can do it with God's help. In fact, we can *only* do it with God's help. Therefore, let's seek His blessing and boldly take our nation back.

THE CONSTITUTION OF THE UNITED STATES

WE THE PEOPLE of the United States, in Order to form a more perfect Union, establish Justice, insure domestic Tranquility, provide for the common defence, promote the general Welfare, and secure the Blessings of Liberty to ourselves and our Posterity, do ordain and establish this Constitution for the United States of America.

ARTICLE I

Section 1. All legislative Powers herein granted shall be vested in a Congress of the United States, which shall consist of a Senate and House of Representatives.

Section 2. The House of Representatives shall be composed of Members chosen every second Year by the People of the several States, and the Electors in each State shall have the Qualifications requisite for Electors of the most numerous Branch of the State Legislature.

No Person shall be a Representative who shall not have attained to the age of twenty five Years, and been seven Years a Citizen of the United States, and who shall not, when elected, be an Inhabitant of that State in which he shall be chosen.

Representatives and direct Taxes shall be apportioned among the several States which may be included within this Union, according to their respective Numbers, which shall be determined by adding to the whole Number of free Persons, including those bound to Service for a Term of Years, and excluding Indians not taxed, three fifths of all other Persons. The actual Enumeration shall be made within three Years after the first Meeting of the Congress of the United States, and within every subsequent Term of ten Years, in such Manner as they shall by Law direct. The Number of Representatives shall not exceed one for every thirty Thousand, but each State shall have at Least one Representative; and until such enumeration shall be made, the State of New Hampshire shall be entitled to chuse three, Massachusetts eight, Rhode-Island and Providence Plantations one, Connecticut five, New-York six, New Jersey four, Pennsylvania eight, Delaware one, Maryland six, Virginia ten, North Carolina five, South Carolina five, and Georgia three.

When vacancies happen in the Representation from any State, the

Executive Authority thereof shall issue Writs of Election to fill such Vacancies.

The House of Representatives shall chuse their Speaker and other Officers; and shall have the sole Power of Impeachment.

Section 3. The Senate of the United States shall be composed of two Senators from each State, chosen by the Legislature thereof, for six Years; and each Senator shall have one Vote.

Immediately after they shall be assembled in Consequence of the first Election, they shall be divided as equally as may be into three Classes. The Seats of the Senators of the first Class shall be vacated at the Expiration of the second Year, of the second Class at the

Expiration of the fourth Year, and the third Class at the Expiration of the sixth Year, so that one third may be chosen every second Year; and if Vacancies happen by Resignation, or otherwise, during the Recess of the Legislature of any State, the Executive thereof may make temporary Appointments until the next Meeting of the Legislature, which shall then fill such Vacancies.

No Person shall be a Senator who shall not have attained to the Age of thirty Years, and been nine Years a Citizen of the United States and who shall not, when elected, be an Inhabitant of that State for which he shall be chosen.

The Vice President of the United States shall be President of the Senate, but shall have no Vote, unless they be equally divided.

The Senate shall chuse their other Officers, and also a President pro tempore, in the Absence of the Vice President, or when he shall exercise the Office of President of the United States.

The Senate shall have the sole Power to try all Impeachments. When sitting for that Purpose, they shall be on Oath or Affirmation. When the President of the United States is tried, the Chief Justice shall preside: And no Person shall be convicted without the Concurrence of two thirds of the Members present.

Judgment in Cases of Impeachment shall not extend further than to removal from Office, and disqualification to hold and enjoy any Office of Honor, Trust or Profit under the United States: but the Party convicted shall nevertheless be liable and subject to Indictment, Trial, Judgment and Punishment, according to Law.

Section 4. The Times, Places and Manner of holding Elections for Senators and Representatives, shall be prescribed in each State by the Legislature thereof; but the Congress may at any time by Law make or alter such Regulations, except as to the Places of chusing Senators.

The Congress shall assemble at least once in every Year, and such Meeting shall be on the first Monday in December, unless they shall by Law appoint a different Day.

Section 5. Each House shall be the Judge of the Elections, Returns and Qualifications of its own Members, and a Majority of each shall constitute a Quorum to do Business; but a smaller Number may adjourn from day to day, and may be authorized to compel the Attendance of absent Members, in such Manner, and under such Penalties as each House may provide.

Each House may determine the Rules of its Proceedings, punish its Members for disorderly Behaviour, and, with the Concurrence of two thirds, expel a Member.

Each House shall keep a Journal of its Proceedings, and from time to time publish the same, excepting such Parts as may in their Judgment require Secrecy; and the Yeas and

Nays of the Members of either House on any question shall, at the Desire of one fifth of those Present, be entered on the Journal.

Neither House, during the Session of Congress, shall, without the Consent of the other, adjourn for more than three days, nor to any other Place than that in which the two Houses shall be sitting.

Section 6. The Senators and Representatives shall receive a Compensation for their Services, to be ascertained by Law, and paid out of the Treasury of the United States. They shall in all Cases, except Treason, Felony and Breach of the Peace, be privileged from Arrest during their Attendance at the Session of their respective Houses, and in going to and returning from the same; and for any Speech or Debate in either House, they shall not be questioned in any other Place.

No Senator or Representative shall, during the Time for which he was elected, be appointed to any civil Office under the Authority of the United States, which shall have been created, or the Emoluments whereof shall have been encreased during such time: and no Person holding any Office under the United States, shall be a Member of either House during his Continuance in Office.

Section 7. All Bills for raising Revenue shall originate in the House of Representatives; but the Senate may propose or concur with Amendments as on other Bills.

Every Bill which shall have passed the House of Representatives and the Senate, shall, before it become a Law, be presented to the President of the United States; if he approve he shall sign it, but if not he shall return it, with his Objections to that House in which it shall have originated, who shall enter the Objections at large on their Journal, and proceed to reconsider it. If after such Reconsideration two thirds of that House shall agree to pass the Bill, it shall be sent, together with the Objections, to the other House, by which it shall likewise be reconsidered, and if approved by two thirds of that House, it shall become a Law. But in all such Cases the Votes of both Houses shall be determined by Yeas and Nays, and the

Names of the Persons voting for and against the Bill shall be entered on the Journal of each House respectively. If any Bill shall not be returned by the President within ten Days (Sundays excepted) after it shall have been presented to him, the Same shall be a Law, in like Manner as if he had signed it, unless the Congress by their Adjournment prevent its Return, in which Case it shall not be a Law.

Every Order, Resolution, or Vote to which the Concurrence of the Senate and House of Representatives may be necessary (except on a question of Adjournment) shall be presented to the President of the United States; and before the Same shall take Effect, shall be approved by him, or being disapproved by him, shall be repassed by two thirds of the Senate and House of Representatives, according to the Rules and Limitations prescribed in the Case of a Bill.

Section 8. The Congress shall have Power To lay and collect Taxes, Duties, Imposts and Excises, to pay the Debts and provide for the common Defence and general Welfare of the United States; but all Duties, Imposts and Excises shall be uniform throughout the United States;

To borrow Money on the credit of the United States;

To regulate Commerce with foreign Nations, and among the several States, and with the Indian Tribes;

To establish an uniform Rule of

Naturalization, and uniform Laws on the subject of Bankruptcies throughout the United States;

To coin Money, regulate the Value thereof, and of foreign Coin, and fix the Standard of Weights and Measures;

To provide for the Punishment of counterfeiting the Securities and current Coin of the United States;

To establish Post Offices and post Roads;

To promote the Progress of Science and useful Arts, by securing for limited Times to Authors and Inventors the exclusive Right to their respective Writings and Discoveries;

To constitute Tribunals inferior to the supreme Court;

To define and punish Piracies and

Felonies committed on the high Seas, and Offences against the Law of Nations;

To declare War, grant Letters of Marque and Reprisal, and make Rules concerning Captures on Land and Water;

To raise and support Armies, but no Appropriation of Money to that Use shall be for a longer Term than two Years;

To provide and maintain a Navy;

To make Rules for the Government and Regulation of the land and naval Forces;

To provide for calling forth the Militia to execute the Laws of the Union, suppress Insurrections and repel Invasions;

To provide for organizing, arming, and disciplining, the Militia, and for governing such Part of them as may be employed in the

Service of the United States, reserving to the States respectively, the Appointment of the Officers, and the Authority of training the Militia according to the discipline prescribed by Congress;

To exercise exclusive Legislation in all Cases whatsoever, over such District (not exceeding ten Miles square) as may, by Cession of particular States, and the Acceptance of Congress, become the Seat of the Government of the United States, and to exercise like Authority over all Places purchased by the Consent of the Legislature of the State in which the Same shall be, for the Erection of Forts, Magazines, Arsenals, dock-Yards, and other needful Buildings;--And

To make all Laws which shall be necessary

and proper for carrying into Execution the foregoing Powers, and all other Powers vested by this Constitution in the Government of the United States, or in any Department or Officer thereof.

Section 9. The Migration or Importation of such Persons as any of the States now existing shall think proper to admit, shall not be prohibited by the Congress prior to the Year one thousand eight hundred and eight, but a Tax or duty may be imposed on such Importation, not exceeding ten dollars for each Person.

The Privilege of the Writ of Habeas Corpus shall not be suspended, unless when in Cases of Rebellion or Invasion the public

Safety may require it.

No Bill of Attainder or ex post facto Law shall be passed.

No Capitation, or other direct, Tax shall be laid, unless in Proportion to the Census or Enumeration herein before directed to be taken.

No Tax or Duty shall be laid on Articles exported from any State.

No Preference shall be given by any Regulation of Commerce or Revenue to the Ports of one State over those of another: nor shall Vessels bound to, or from, one State, be obliged to enter, clear or pay Duties in another.

No Money shall be drawn from the Treasury, but in Consequence of

Appropriations made by Law; and a regular Statement and Account of Receipts and Expenditures of all public Money shall be published from time to time.

No Title of Nobility shall be granted by the United States: And no Person holding any Office of Profit or Trust under them, shall, without the Consent of the Congress, accept of any present, Emolument, Office, or Title, of any kind whatever, from any King, Prince, or foreign State.

Section 10. No State shall enter into any Treaty, Alliance, or Confederation; grant Letters of Marque and Reprisal; coin Money; emit Bills of Credit; make any Thing but gold and silver Coin a Tender in Payment of Debts; pass any Bill of Attainder, ex post facto Law, or Law impairing the Obligation of Contracts, or grant any Title of Nobility.

No State shall, without the Consent of the Congress, lay any Imposts or Duties on Imports or Exports, except what may be absolutely necessary for executing it's inspection Laws: and the net Produce of all Duties and Imposts, laid by any State on Imports or Exports, shall be for the Use of the Treasury of the United States; and all such Laws shall be subject to the Revision and Controul of the Congress.

No State shall, without the Consent of Congress, lay any Duty of Tonnage, keep Troops, or Ships of War in time of Peace, enter into any Agreement or Compact with another State, or with a foreign Power, or engage in War, unless actually invaded, or in such imminent Danger as will not admit of delay.

ARTICLE II

Section 1. The executive Power shall be vested in a President of the United States of America. He shall hold his Office during the Term of four Years, and, together with the Vice President, chosen for the same Term, be elected, as follows:

Each State shall appoint, in such Manner as the Legislature thereof may direct, a Number of Electors, equal to the whole

Number of Senators and Representatives to which the State may be entitled in the Congress: but no Senator or Representative, or Person holding an Office of Trust or Profit under the United States, shall be appointed an Elector.

The Electors shall meet in their respective States, and vote by Ballot for two Persons, of whom one at least shall not be an Inhabitant of the same State with themselves. And they shall make a List of all the Persons voted for, and of the Number of Votes for each; which List they shall sign and certify, and transmit sealed to the Seat of the Government of the United States, directed to the President of the Senate. The President of the Senate shall, in the Presence of the Senate and House of

Representatives, open all the Certificates, and the Votes shall then be counted. The Person having the greatest Number of Votes shall be the President, if such Number be a Majority of the whole Number of Electors appointed; and if there be more than one who have such Majority, and have an equal Number of Votes, then the House of Representatives shall immediately chuse by Ballot one of them for President; and if no Person have a Majority, then from the five highest on the List the said House shall in like Manner chuse the President. But in chusing the President, the Votes shall be taken by States, the Representation from each State having one Vote; A quorum for this Purpose shall consist of a Member or

Members from two thirds of the States, and a Majority of all the States shall be necessary to a Choice. In every Case, after the Choice of the President, the Person having the greatest Number of Votes of the Electors shall be the Vice President. But if there should remain two or more who have equal Votes, the Senate shall chuse from them by Ballot the Vice President.

The Congress may determine the Time of chusing the Electors, and the Day on which they shall give their Votes; which Day shall be the same throughout the United States.

No Person except a natural born Citizen, or a Citizen of the United States, at the time of the Adoption of this Constitution, shall be eligible to the Office of President;

neither shall any Person be eligible to that Office who shall not have attained to the Age of thirty five Years, and been fourteen Years a Resident within the United States.

In Case of the Removal of the President from Office, or of his Death, Resignation, or Inability to discharge the Powers and Duties of the said Office, the Same shall devolve on the Vice President, and the Congress may by Law provide for the Case of Removal, Death, Resignation or Inability, both of the President and Vice President, declaring what Officer shall then act as President, and such Officer shall act accordingly, until the Disability be removed, or a President shall be elected.

The President shall, at stated Times, receive for his Services, a Compensation, which shall neither be encreased nor diminished during the Period for which he shall have been elected, and he shall not receive within that Period any other Emolument from the United States, or any of them.

Before he enter on the Execution of his Office, he shall take the following Oath or Affirmation:--"I do solemnly swear (or affirm) that I will faithfully execute the Office of President of the United States, and will to the best of my Ability, preserve, protect and defend the Constitution of the United States."

Section 2. The President shall be Commander in Chief of the Army and Navy of the United States, and of the Militia of the several States, when called into the actual Service of the United States; he may require the Opinion, in writing, of the principal Officer in each of the executive Departments, upon any Subject relating to the Duties of their respective Offices, and he shall have Power to grant Reprieves and Pardons for Offences against the United States, except in Cases of Impeachment.

He shall have Power, by and with the Advice and Consent of the Senate, to make Treaties, provided two thirds of the Senators present concur; and he shall nominate, and by and with the Advice and Consent of the Senate, shall appoint Ambassadors, other public Ministers and Consuls, Judges of the supreme Court, and all other Officers of the United States, whose Appointments are not herein otherwise provided for, and which shall be established by Law: but the Congress may by Law vest the Appointment of such inferior Officers, as they think proper, in the President alone, in the Courts of Law, or in the Heads of Departments.

The President shall have Power to fill up all Vacancies that may happen during the Recess of the Senate, by granting Commissions which shall expire at the End of their next Session.

Section 3. He shall from time to time give to the Congress Information of the State of the Union, and recommend to their

Consideration such Measures as he shall judge necessary and expedient; he may, on extraordinary Occasions, convene both Houses, or either of them, and in Case of Disagreement between them, with Respect to the Time of Adjournment, he may adjourn them to such Time as he shall think proper; he shall receive Ambassadors and other public Ministers; he shall take Care that the Laws be faithfully executed, and shall Commission all the Officers of the United States.

Section 4. The President, Vice President and all civil Officers of the United States, shall be removed from Office on Impeachment for, and Conviction of, Treason, Bribery, or other high Crimes and Misdemeanors.

ARTICLE III

Section 1. The judicial Power of the United States, shall be vested in one supreme Court, and in such inferior Courts as the Congress may from time to time ordain and establish. The Judges, both of the supreme and inferior Courts, shall hold their Offices during good Behaviour, and shall, at stated Times, receive for their Services, a Compensation, which shall not be diminished during their Continuance in Office.

Section 2. The judicial Power shall extend to all Cases, in Law and Equity, arising under this Constitution, the Laws of the United States, and Treaties made, or which

shall be made, under their Authority;--
to all Cases affecting Ambassadors, other
public Ministers and Consuls;--to all Cases
of admiralty and maritime Jurisdiction;--
to Controversies to which the United States
shall be a Party;--to Controversies between
two or more States;--between a State and
Citizens of another State;--between Citizens
of different States;--between Citizens of
the same State claiming Lands under Grants
of different States, and between a State, or
the Citizens thereof, and foreign States,
Citizens or Subjects.

In all Cases affecting Ambassadors, other
public Ministers and Consuls, and those in
which a State shall be Party, the supreme
Court shall have original Jurisdiction. In

all the other Cases before mentioned, the supreme Court shall have appellate Jurisdiction, both as to Law and Fact, with such Exceptions, and under such Regulations as the Congress shall make.

The Trial of all Crimes, except in Cases of Impeachment, shall be by Jury; and such Trial shall be held in the State where the said Crimes shall have been committed; but when not committed within any State, the Trial shall be at such Place or Places as the Congress may by Law have directed.

Section 3. Treason against the United States, shall consist only in levying War against them, or in adhering to their Enemies, giving them Aid and Comfort. No Person shall be convicted of Treason unless on the Testimony of two Witnesses to the same overt Act, or on Confession in open Court.

The Congress shall have Power to declare the Punishment of Treason, but no Attainder of Treason shall work Corruption of Blood, or Forfeiture except during the Life of the Person attainted.

ARTICLE IV

Section 1. Full Faith and Credit shall be given in each State to the public Acts, Records, and judicial Proceedings of every other State. And the Congress may by general Laws prescribe the Manner in which such Acts, Records, and Proceedings shall be proved, and the Effect thereof.

Section 2. The Citizens of each State shall be entitled to all Privileges and Immunities of Citizens in the several States.

A Person charged in any State with Treason, Felony, or other Crime, who shall flee from Justice, and be found in another State, shall on Demand of the executive Authority of the State from which he fled, be delivered up, to be removed to the State having Jurisdiction of the Crime.

No Person held to Service or Labour in one State, under the Laws thereof, escaping into another, shall, in Consequence of any Law or Regulation therein, be discharged from such Service or Labour, but shall be delivered up on Claim of the Party to whom such Service or Labour may be due.

Section 3. New States may be admitted by the Congress into this Union; but no new States shall be formed or erected within the Jurisdiction of any other State; nor any State be formed by the Junction of two or more States, or Parts of States, without the Consent of the Legislatures of the States concerned as well as of the Congress.

The Congress shall have Power to dispose of and make all needful Rules and Regulations respecting the Territory or other Property belonging to the United States; and nothing in this Constitution shall be so construed as to Prejudice any Claims of the United States, or of any particular State.

Section 4. The United States shall guarantee to every State in this Union a Republican Form of Government, and shall protect each of them against Invasion; and on Application of the Legislature, or of the Executive (when the Legislature cannot be convened) against domestic Violence.

ARTICLE V

The Congress, whenever two thirds of both Houses shall deem it necessary, shall propose Amendments to this Constitution, or, on the

Application of the Legislatures of two thirds of the several States, shall call a Convention for proposing Amendments, which, in either Case, shall be valid to all Intents and Purposes, as Part of this Constitution, when ratified by the Legislatures of three fourths of the several States, or by Conventions in three fourths thereof, as the one or the other Mode of Ratification may be proposed by the Congress; Provided that no Amendment which may be made prior to the Year One thousand eight hundred and eight shall in any Manner affect the first and fourth Clauses in the Ninth Section of the first Article; and that no State, without its Consent, shall be deprived of its equal Suffrage in the Senate.

All Debts contracted and Engagements entered into, before the Adoption of this Constitution, shall be as valid against the United States under this Constitution, as under the Confederation.

This Constitution, and the Laws of the United States which shall be made in Pursuance thereof; and all Treaties made, or which shall be made, under the Authority of the United States, shall be the supreme Law of the Land; and the Judges in every State shall be bound thereby, any Thing in the Constitution or Laws of any State to the Contrary notwith-standing.

The Senators and Representatives before

mentioned, and the Members of the several State Legislatures, and all executive and judicial Officers, both of the United States and of the several States, shall be bound by Oath or Affirmation, to support this Constitution; but no religious Test shall ever be required as a Qualification to any Office or public Trust under the United States.

ARTICLE VII

The Ratification of the Conventions of nine States, shall be sufficient for the Establishment of this Constitution between the States so ratifying the Same.

Done in Convention by the Unanimous

Consent of the States present the Seventeenth Day of September in the Year of our Lord one thousand seven hundred and Eighty seven and of the Independence of the United States of America the Twelfth

In witness whereof We have hereunto subscribed our Names,

George Washington--President and deputy from Virginia

New Hampshire: John Langdon, Nicholas Gilman

Massachusetts: Nathaniel Gorham, Rufus King

Connecticut: William Samuel Johnson, Roger Sherman

New York: Alexander Hamilton

New Jersey: William Livingston, David Brearly,

William Paterson, Jonathan Dayton

Pennsylvania: Benjamin Franklin, Thomas Mifflin, Robert Morris, George Clymer, Thomas FitzSimons, Jared Ingersoll, James Wilson, Gouverneur Morris

Delaware: George Read, Gunning Bedford, Jr., John Dickinson, Richard Bassett, Jacob Broom

Maryland: James McHenry, Daniel of Saint Thomas Jenifer, Daniel Carroll

Virginia: John Blair, James Madison, Jr.

North Carolina: William Blount, Richard Dobbs Spaight, Hugh Williamson

South Carolina: John Rutledge, Charles Cotesworth Pinckney, Charles Pinckney, Pierce Butler

Georgia: William Few, Abraham Baldwin

THE DECLARATION OF INDEPENDENCE

IN CONGRESS, July 4, 1776.

The unanimous Declaration of the thirteen united States of America,

When in the Course of human events, it becomes necessary for one people to dissolve the political bands which have connected them with another, and to assume among the powers of the earth, the separate and equal station to which the Laws of Nature and of Nature's God entitle them, a decent respect to the opinions of mankind requires that they should declare the causes which impel them to the separation.

We hold these truths to be self-evident, that all men are created equal, that they are endowed by their Creator with certain unalienable Rights, that among these are Life, Liberty and the pursuit of Happiness.--That to secure these rights, Governments are instituted among Men, deriving their just powers from the consent of the governed, --That whenever any Form of Government becomes destructive of these ends, it is the

Right of the People to alter or to abolish it, and to institute new Government, laying its foundation on such principles and organizing its powers in such form, as to them shall seem most likely to effect their Safety and Happiness. Prudence, indeed, will dictate that Governments long established should not be changed for light and transient causes; and accordingly all experience hath shewn, that mankind are more disposed to suffer, while evils are sufferable, than to right themselves by abolishing the forms to which they are accustomed. But when a long train of abuses and usurpations, pursuing invariably the same Object evinces a design to reduce them under absolute Despotism, it is their right, it is their duty, to throw off such

Government, and to provide new Guards for their future security.--Such has been the patient sufferance of these Colonies; and such is now the necessity which constrains them to alter their former Systems of Government. The history of the present King of Great Britain is a history of repeated injuries and usurpations, all having in direct object the establishment of an absolute Tyranny over these States. To prove this, let Facts be submitted to a candid world.

He has refused his Assent to Laws, the most wholesome and necessary for the public good.

He has forbidden his Governors to pass Laws of immediate and pressing importance, unless suspended in their operation till his Assent should be obtained; and when so suspended, he has utterly neglected to attend to them.

He has refused to pass other Laws for the accommodation of large districts of people, unless those people would relinquish the right of Representation in the Legislature, a right inestimable to them and formidable to tyrants only.

He has called together legislative bodies at places unusual, uncomfortable, and distant from the depository of their public Records, for the sole purpose of fatiguing them into compliance with his measures.

He has dissolved Representative Houses repeatedly, for opposing with manly firmness his invasions on the rights of the people.

He has refused for a long time, after such dissolutions, to cause others to be elected; whereby the Legislative powers, incapable of Annihilation, have returned to the People at large for their exercise; the State remaining in the mean time exposed to all the dangers of invasion from without, and convulsions within.

He has endeavoured to prevent the population of these States; for that purpose obstructing the Laws for Naturalization of Foreigners; refusing to pass others to encourage their migrations hither, and raising the conditions of new Appropriations of Lands.

He has obstructed the Administration of Justice, by refusing his Assent to Laws for establishing Judiciary powers.

He has made Judges dependent on his Will alone, for the tenure of their offices, and the amount and payment of their salaries.

He has erected a multitude of New Offices, and sent hither swarms of Officers to harrass our people, and eat out their substance.

He has kept among us, in times of peace, Standing Armies without the Consent of our legislatures.

He has affected to render the Military independent of and superior to the Civil power.

He has combined with others to subject us to a jurisdiction foreign to our constitution, and unacknowledged by our laws; giving his Assent to their Acts of pretended Legislation:

For Quartering large bodies of armed troops among us:

For protecting them, by a mock Trial, from punishment for any Murders which they should commit on the Inhabitants of these States:

For cutting off our Trade with all parts of the world:

For imposing Taxes on us without our Consent:

For depriving us in many cases, of the benefits of Trial by Jury:

For transporting us beyond Seas to be tried for pretended offences

For abolishing the free System of English Laws in a neighbouring Province, establishing therein an Arbitrary government, and enlarging its Boundaries so as to render it at once an example and fit instrument for introducing the same absolute rule into these Colonies:

For taking away our Charters, abolishing our most valuable Laws, and altering fundamentally the Forms of our Governments:

For suspending our own Legislatures, and declaring themselves invested with power to legislate for us in all cases whatsoever.

He has abdicated Government here, by declaring us out of his Protection and waging War against us.

He has plundered our seas, ravaged our Coasts, burnt our towns, and destroyed the lives of our people.

He is at this time transporting large Armies of foreign Mercenaries to compleat the works of death, desolation and tyranny, already begun with circumstances of Cruelty & perfidy scarcely paralleled in the most barbarous ages, and totally unworthy the Head of a civilized nation.

He has constrained our fellow Citizens taken Captive on the high Seas to bear Arms against their Country, to become the executioners of their friends and Brethren, or to fall themselves by their Hands.

He has excited domestic insurrections amongst us, and has endeavoured to bring on the inhabitants of our frontiers, the merciless Indian Savages, whose known rule of warfare, is an undistinguished destruction of all ages, sexes and conditions.

In every stage of these Oppressions We have Petitioned for Redress in the most humble terms: Our repeated Petitions have been answered only by repeated injury. A Prince whose character is thus marked by every act which may define a Tyrant, is unfit to be the ruler of a free people.

Nor have We been wanting in attentions to our Brittish brethren. We have warned them from time to time of attempts by their legislature to extend an unwarrantable jurisdiction over us. We have reminded them of the circumstances of our emigration and settlement here. We have appealed to their native justice and magnanimity, and we have conjured them by the ties of our common kindred to disavow these usurpations, which, would inevitably interrupt our connections and correspondence. They too have been deaf to the voice of justice and of consanguinity. We must, therefore, acquiesce in the necessity, which denounces our Separation, and hold them, as we hold the rest of mankind, Enemies in War, in Peace Friends.

We, therefore, the Representatives of the united States of America, in General Congress, Assembled, appealing to the Supreme Judge of the world for the rectitude of our intentions, do, in the Name, and by Authority of the good People of these Colonies, solemnly publish and declare, That these United Colonies are, and of Right ought to be Free and Independent

States; that they are Absolved from all Allegiance to the British Crown, and that all political connection between them and the State of Great Britain, is and ought to be totally dissolved; and that as Free and Independent States, they have full Power to levy War, conclude Peace, contract Alliances, establish Commerce, and to do all other Acts and Things which Independent States may of right do. And for the support of this Declaration, with a firm reliance on the protection of divine Providence, we mutually pledge to each other our Lives, our Fortunes and our sacred Honor.